WHAT ARE YOU GIVING BACK TO THE COMMUNITY?

A Public-Private Real Estate Development Manual

By Jerrod Delaine

What Are You Giving Back to the Community? A Public-Private Real Estate Development Manual © 2020 Jerrod Delaine

All Rights Reserved

CONTENTS

INTRODUCTION

FINANCE

CONSTRUCTION

DESIGN

CONCLUSION

CLOSING THOUGHTS

GLOSSARY

INTRODUCTION

About the Author

In 2003, I completed my Bachelor of Science in Architecture from Florida Agricultural & Mechanical University. I went to work in a design firm for a few years focused mostly on multifamily buildings in the southeast region of the United States. In 2012, I completed my Master of Science in Real Estate Development from New York University. I am a practicing real estate development professional and college professor in New York City.

About the Book Series

The field of real estate development is complicated. I am breaking this complex topic into a series of small books; this book is the fourth.

On occasion, I receive requests from professionals who want to know how this real estate development business works. A significant portion of the population that doesn't even know this field exists.

The purpose of this book series is to provide a brief introduction to this exciting industry. This industry is financially fulfilling when done successfully. But even more importantly, the decisions made as a practicing real estate industry professional can make an impact on communities that lasts for generations.

This material will also serve as reference materials for currently practicing real estate development professionals.

What is the intent of this book?

This small book is the definitive source to inform you about Public-Private Real Estate Development. I'm also giving you the list of tools to execute these projects successfully.

Who is this book for?

This book is for all of the general public from all social and economic backgrounds. A significant portion of the population does not understand real estate development or public-private real estate development. You will complete this book with a new curiosity to learn more and hopefully find a path that interests you. You'll leave this book with a curiosity about the built environment in your community. In this book, when you see something interesting, feel free to stop and search online about that topic to learn more, then come back to continue the journey. This book will be the springboard to launch you into an exciting new path.

What is Real Estate Development?

Real estate development is the creation of value for real property. The simple and straightforward example of value creation is buying a piece of land and constructing a new building. The value creation that entertains people on television is purchasing a dilapidated house, renovating it and selling it for a quick profit. Creating value this way is not nearly as easy as shown on media outlets. A more complicated value creation example is buying an existing building in a densely-populated neighborhood and increasing the rental income while reducing expenses.

What is Public-Private Real Estate Development?

Public-Private Real Estate Development occurs when public entities and private developers work together using their resources for a common goal. Some of the specific objectives are creating/preserving affordable housing, spur economic development, creating jobs, and providing high-quality education facilities. The public party typically wants to use its resources to achieve the best outcome possible. The private party wants to achieve a risk adjusted profit by providing a service that the community needs. The private party brings capital in the form of equity and debt capacity. The private party also brings along the ability to raise equity and debt from passive investors who want a return on investment while achieving public goals. A successful public-private project occurs when the public receives its desired deliverables, and the private parties complete the service with a return on investment. In some cases, it also gains a long term stream of income.

OVERVIEW

I am filled with so much joy teaching this topic as a college course. There are always new anecdotes and a constant barrage of unknown variables. For example, Amazon and its search for a headquarters were a source of spirited conversation in my class, which peaked when they chose New York City. When had great conversations when the Amazon HQ search reached a fascinating conclusion as the agreement dramatical collapsed. That was a prominent example, a more subtle example is you or I buying a small property in a new community, that community can help or hurt our proposed change to their community. My suggestion is not to shy away from this moment, but engage. You must offer something of value to the community, give back. You are blessed to have access to resources and (hopefully) knowledge that can mold communities. I implore you. Use that power for good.

PUBLIC-PRIVATE REAL ESTATE DEVELOPMENT PROJECT TYPES

I'm not suggesting you'll be able to go out and finance a highway or charter school after this book. But you will understand the approach, why it's a good idea to do a public-private project, and desired outcomes for all involved.

I will spend a good part of this book discussing housing; shelter is a fundamental need for cities to create, provide, and preserve continually.

Schools are a public necessity. The private market could provide new and innovative solutions in a manner that is faster and more agile than the Department of Education. As an educator, I can tell you firsthand that everyone does not learn the same. Our education system and facilities should be able to adjust to our young peoples' needs.

Infrastructure projects such as bridges and highways are an integral part of cities. It's the artery through which food, goods, services, and people circulate.

Offices are the center of employment and economic productivity. Some municipalities have a particular industry that is a significant economic driver, such as tech in Silicon Valley, government policy in Washington DC, healthcare and research in Boston, oil commodities in Texas, and finance in New York City.

Retail space provides the source of food in communities. Cities can choose to either allow unhealthy food providers to overtake communities or instead can incentivize food providers to invest in foods, goods, and services that encourage and foster healthy eating and habits. This choice directly impacts the life and health of the community.

Speaking of healthy, many towns and communities are encouraging their residents to partake in other facets of healthy living, such as outdoor exercise and activities. Including bike trails, running paths and hiking trails, and area to enjoy outdoors improve communities on various levels. They promote cardiovascular health, increased property values, reduced vehicular congestion, and pollution. On a bike or running, exploring a new community is often far superior experience and feel compared to a car or public transportation. The best cities in the world know this and integrate that into their city planning.

BENEFITS AND RISKS

Public-Private Partnerships facilitate a scenario where benefits and risks can be strategical to accomplish goals. Public parties can tap those private resources to achieve the desired outcome, like workforce housing and workforce training. The government also can achieve those goals without outlaying their cash. Private investments increase the capacity and expand the possibilities. This strategy also protects the public from the downside of investments, losing money in economic downturns. Simultaneously, public participants such as finance agencies and city planners can sit in the driver's seat steering community change. Private parties also bring efficiencies and management staff; this provides a different motivation and decision making tree.

FINANCE

When we have the vision to create something extraordinary, the critical initial question is, how do we pay for it? This question you or your team should ask yourself at the beginning of the process.

EQUITY

The first question you may have is, "what is equity anyway?" Equity is the value of an asset less the liabilities on that asset. Equity is one's ownership stake in investments after all loans. For example, if you own a home worth $100,000, but have a mortgage balance of $80,000, you have an equity value or real property value of $20,000.

Private Investment

Private developers bring equity to these deals as a pivotal piece to the puzzle. Developers can provide capital as a part of their capabilities. Private investors and developers also raise money from the private market place.

Private capital brings its expertise and management prowess to the project. The benefits from this could include increased collected revenue with existing tenants.

Private parties could also reduce operating expresses through facilities, repairs, consolidation, and optimization. Private capital also can use leverage to minimize cash needed while maximizing returns,

Cryptocurrency

Although still in its infant stage and highly volatile, cryptocurrency has potential. I would like to note that the idea of a digital/non-centralized authority/virtual currency, tied with an online tracking system has incredible potential. The ledger, or blockchain technology, keeps an online log of transaction data in a manner more efficient than some small countries. Developing or emerging countries could harness this investment vehicle to bring capital into lacking financial interests.

Crowd Funding

The crowdfunding platform has gained a lot of popularity in recent years. Crowdfunding is a way to raise money from many investors on an online platform for the desired project. Using this specifically for real estate expanded once the Title III section of the JOBS Act established the regulatory framework for raising capital through security offerings utilizing the crowdfunding platform. The

Jumpstart Our Business Start-Ups Act, or JOBS Act, is a federal law seeking to encourage small business funding through the alteration of traditional regulations. Like the stock market, anyone can invest in crowdfunding platforms, which is exciting as it may democratize the investment space. Like other parts of society, technology is moving faster than our systems can keep up with, crowdfunding is a new space with exponential growth potential.

Government Equity

The government can provide equity tools to assist in the success. Tax credits have been a phenomenal tool utilized in a variety of formats.

Low Income Housing Tax Credits

Low Income Housing Tax Credits (LIHTC) have had an incredibly successful run in creating and preserving affordable housing in America.

LIHTC has created over 2 million residential homes since its creation. This program provides a tax incentive for investors to place their capital into rental housing for low-income households. These tax credit investors and tax-exempt bonds fund the acquisition, construction, renovations, and related costs needed for affordable development projects.

LIHTC is a complicated deal structure. I'll try to explain it quickly. The government provides a qualified developer with tax credits for the project. The developer then takes those tax credits and sell them to an investor; those investors will provide cash in exchange for the tax credits, some of the massive tax credit purchasers are banks and insurance companies. I was once involved with a project where the tax credit purchaser was a large oil company. Those companies have internal controls that help determine how much the tax credits are worth to their organization.

The developer takes that cash and invests it into the affordable real estate development project. They are required to stay in compliance with the rules and regulations for ten years.

The combination of cash from the tax credits and the tax-exempt bond debt provide the capital to develop the project. When there is a gap, the developer can provide the needed capital or the government could provide additional subsidies to help fund the project.

New Market Tax Credits

The New Market Tax Credit (NMTC) program provides a financial tool to incentivize commercial space investment for underserved communities. The NMTC was created under the Community Renewal and Tax Relief Act of 2000.

This program is administered by the Internal Revenue Service (IRS) and Community Development Financial Institutions (CFDIs). This program is created to break the cycle of disinvestment. The intent is to attract capital to underinvested communities. This lack of investment manifests through vacant commercial properties, underutilized industrial buildings, and less than optimal healthcare facilities. NMTC provides a credit against federal income taxes for investors that make Qualified Equity Investments in Community Development Entities.

Historic Tax Credits

Historic tax credits are a tool to encourage the preservation of historically relevant buildings. Unfortunately, there are instances where the cost to renovate the building may not be feasible in older facilities. The government provides this tool to encourage the investment and redevelopment of existing buildings that are historically important to the community, city, state, or nation.

Public Companies and Real Estate Investment Trusts

Public Companies are corporations whose ownership is distributed to general public shareholders with shares of stock on exchanges. Public companies have access to equity and debt facilities.

Real Estate Investment Trusts (REITs) are companies that own or finance income-producing real estate. REITs trade on the major stock exchanges. REITs typically specialize by property type, including but not limited to Industrial/Office, Retail, Diversified, Residential, Lodging/Resorts, HealthCare, Self Storage, and Specialty. Investors like REITs because this investment vehicle provides a safe way to invest in real estate interests, in exchange for a consistent return on investment through dividends. Online platforms allow anyone to create a profile with less than $100, and in minutes that person can own stock in a real estate investment trust. REITs enjoy the liquidity of the public markets.

The United States Security and Exchange Commission or SEC, sets reporting requirements, establish rules, and enforces laws with public companies on behalf of the public.

In 2015, a large asset management firm called Blackstone Group purchased a large residential community in lower Manhattan called Stuyvesant Town-Peter Cooper Village (Stuytown). The purchase price was $5.3 billion. Blackstone has access to both equity and debt on the public stock exchange, and a REIT platform, which gives them incredible access to capital to do great things. Under the terms of the Stuytown deal, out of a total of 11,250 apartments, Blackstone will keep 5,000 apartments affordable for residents for 20 years. The city of New York will also contribute incentives toward the affordability of this large residential complex. The Blackstone investment into Stuytown is an excellent example of harnessing public markets to preserve affordable housing.

DEBT

You may be asking yourself, what exactly is debt? Debt is also known as leverage. Leverage is the sword of capitalism. When this tool is employed correctly, you gain extraordinary financial capabilities. Leverage allows borrowers to spread risk.

Private Debt

The private parties can utilize commercial lending vehicles to achieve the desired results. Lenders such as Wells Fargo, Citibank, and many other lenders provide loan products focused on community development initiatives. These initiatives include affordable housing, education facilities, and small business space.

Public Debt

The public markets purchase tax except for municipal bonds. Citizens invest in bonds seeking reliable future dividends and returns. The government will direct those funds to the applicable project and manage it from start to completion.

INCENTIVES

Subsidies

One of the common ways in which governments encourage investment from private parties is the use of subsidies. Subsidies are a benefit given to a business by the government in exchange for promoting some public good. For example, the developer must achieve a specific profit to justify building affordable housing, an office complex, or a school. The city may provide subsidies in the form of a mortgage to aid in the capital required to complete the project successfully. Subsidies can come in many ways, such as cash, loans, and tax reduction. Some debt is forgivable if the developers maintain the public good for a designated number of years. The government participants are motivated to deploy government funds to receive the desired outcomes thoughtfully.

Underutilized Public Assets

The government could use its available assets to encourage real estate development. Those assets include vacant land and vacant buildings. Underutilized assets may also consist of unused air rights over low scale buildings and train lines.

Tax Abatements

Real estate taxes are typically one of the highest expenses for those who own real estate. By reducing or removing real estate taxes, the project will more profitable and more valuable. Eliminating real estate taxes is a standard method for the government to encourage developers to provide a service.

Some cities and states apply what's called a PILOT program, which stands for Payments In Lieu Of Taxes. In simple terms, it means the property owner/developer agrees to pay some amount of reduced real estate taxes. For example, a developer may pursue a PILOT in a city because they build or buy a senior housing building. That business model relies on a steady income and ongoing expenses over a long term period.

Zoning

Some communities use zoning as a tool to affect positive change. A city planning department may determine that a particular area in town should be the area designated to be the new high-density residential district. In that scenario, planners could increase the height, lot coverage, and square feet (floor area ratio). In many urban cities, they now have industrial complexes that are underutilized and vacant. For example, in Boston, they changed the zoning to allow more commercial and residential uses in these historically industrial areas, thus dramatically changing that area.

Mortgage Interest Deduction

Mortgage Interest Deduction has been a long celebrated benefit and incentive related to owning a home in America. The mortgage interest deduction provides the homeowners with the ability to deduct the interest they pay on their mortgage, from their income. This deduction can be applied to a person's primary home, second home, and investment properties.

1031 Property Exchange

The 1031 Exchange Program is a prevalent investment tool; its name is from Section 1031 of the U.S. Internal Revenue Code. This government program encourages investment in real estate. It allows an investor to sell their real estate asset, and if they reinvest into another similar real estate asset, they can defer the payment taxes on the profits from the sale. Those taxes are deferred until its time to sell the new investment.

Federal Housing Authority

The home mortgage business has had direct involvement from the federal government for many decades. The Federal government created the Federal Housing

Administration or FHA loan program. In this program, lenders are motivated to allow low down payment, low closing costs, and friendlier credit qualifications. There were many flaws in this system, initially including the exclusion of African American applicants, I'll cover this topic in detail in different publications.

Rehabilitation loans are a creative way to encourage investments. Another type of FHA loan is the FHA 203(k) loan promotes the purchase of existing multifamily homes of 2-4 units explicitly. This loan addresses a significant issue. Many lenders do not want to approve mortgages for a home that needs substantial repairs. With this program, purchasers can receive up to 97% of the renovated value in a loan. The purchaser would need a 3% down to close. The purchaser can use the loan funds to acquire the property and make renovations to that newly purchased real estate asset.

PROFITS AND RETURNS

Private parties would not participate in this line of business if it did not also make a profit. Let's discuss a few of the measures of profitability or returns on investments.

Cash on Cash Returns

Cash on cash represents the return of an investment on an ongoing annual basis. Very often, the government-financed projects require private party involvement in the project for a long term period. Cash on cash return is a reliable measure of how the investment is doing over the years. This return calculates the cash flow for a year divided by the equity invested. For example, if you received an annual cash flow of $100,000 in year two and invested $1,000,000, the cash on cash return in year 2 is 10%. That also means, if constant every year, it will take ten years to receive a return on investment.

Equity Multiple

Equity Multiple is a simplified look at profit. Equity multiple looks at the return on the investment but analyzing the equity invested against the equity profit. For example, if you invest $1,000,000 into a project, if the profit after all funds (equity and debt) is paid back is $1,000,000. You could calculate the EM by equity invested ($1M) plus net profit($1M), divided by equity invested($1M) equals the EM $1M+$1M/$1M = 2.0

Another important factor to point out, this measure of return does not factor in time. So you could receive your profit in a year or ten years and receive the same equity multiple.

CONSTRUCTION

For a long time, construction jobs have been a reliable source of economic development for cities across America. Infrastructure projects such as roads and highways provide years of contracts for contractors and employment for individuals.

GREEN CONSTRUCTION

Many of today's government financing entities require some level of green construction or sustainability when utilizing public funds. According to the United States Green Building Council, green building is a holistic concept that starts with the understanding that the built environment can have profound effects, both positive and negative, on the natural environment, as well as the people who inhabit buildings every day.

Currently, the popular sustainable certifications are LEED, Green Communities, and Energy Star. Leaders in Energy and Environmental Design or LEED is the premier sustainability certification in the world. Enterprise Green Communities is a slightly easier method of achieving a sustainable certification. The Enterprise Green Communities Criteria (EGCC) is a comprehensive nationwide framework designed specifically for green affordable housing. The criteria provide cost-effective standards for creating healthy and energy-efficient buildings. Energy Star is a program run by the U.S. Environmental Protection Agency (EPA) and the U.S. Department of Energy (DOE); this program promotes energy efficiency. ENERGY STAR tools and resources help businesses identify cost-effective approaches to managing energy use in their buildings. The program's popular online tool, ENERGY STAR Portfolio Manager, was used to measure and track the energy, water, and waste. LEED focuses on the effects of the building on the environment; the WELL certification focuses on the building's effects on us humans. The International WELL Building Institute (IWBI) iş leading the global movement to transform our buildings and communities to help people thrive. The International WELL Building Standard is one of the leading global rating systems and the first to be focused exclusively on how buildings can improve our comfort, drive better choices, and generally enhance our health and wellness. In the post COVID world, we will see a more significant focus on healthy buildings.

ECONOMIC DEVELOPMENT

The government can use its capital resources to encourage economic development in specific parts of the community. These targeted measures could create business growth and local hiring, which has a multiplier effect on other elements, such as regional consumer spending, local food, and beverage spending, homeownership, and education. One way to do this is to encourage the growth of Minority and Women Business Enterprise (MWBE) companies. Many government entities are now requiring MBE, WBE, or MWBE participation when performing construction paid for by taxpayer dollars. The construction industry has had a history of excluding certain portions of the population, while the tax dollar arrives from all of the community. To qualify for this certification, as a minority and or women-owned business enterprise, a company must successfully demonstrate that they are independently owned, operated, and controlled by minority members and or women. The ownership must be real and show that the minority members and or women exercise the authority to control day-to-day business decisions independently.

For example, the state of New York state set a guideline for 30% MWBE utilization on projects financed by the government. In total, MWBEs won more than $2.93 billion in state contracts during the 2018-2019 Fiscal Year. This announcement is in conjunction with New York State's ninth annual MWBE Forum, which brings together thousands of business owners, community leaders, state officials, and contractors' representatives to discuss state contracting opportunities and learn about resources available MWBEs. "In New York, we know that diversity is a strength, not a weakness — and when we empower minority and women-owned businesses to compete for state contracts, we create a better New York for all," Governor Andrew Cuomo (MWBE Forum, 2019).

On the federal level, the U.S. Department of Transportation (DOT) developed the Disadvantaged Business Enterprise (DBE) Certification to assist DBE companies that wish to compete for federally funded highway, transit, airport, and highway safety contracts. The state or local governments that receive DOT funding must maintain a DBE program that conforms to DOT standards. A DBE business must be in a socially and economically disadvantaged group and own 51% or more of a small business.

In this manner, DOT is encouraging the growth of small businesses from other portions of the population, not just parties who have historically successfully secured government contracts.

LABOR

Union Vs Non-Union Vs Prevailing Wage Vs. Davis Bacon

Specific government funding programs state the requirements regarding the hiring of contractors and subcontractors. The typical government contract often discussed are Union labor and Prevailing Wage.

Union workers tend to have better access to paid sick days and healthcare. Unions also tend to have internal training programs that require their members to maintain the highest quality of construction means and methods. Union laborers tend to come with a significantly higher hourly rate; therefore, affordable housing tends to use non-union labor.

Prevailing wage is related to the pay rate that contractors and vendors must offer their employees when doing business with government entities. The Davis-Bacon and Related Acts add pay rate requirements to contractors and subcontractors performing on federally funded public works buildings or projects.

When Davis Bacon is applicable, the contractor cannot pay less than the stated prevailing wage and fringe benefits.

Contractors and subcontractors are required to submit certified payrolls to the related government agency; their payrolls show data such as role, hourly rate, hours worked, and if that person is a member of a minority class. For example, in Los Angeles, you must use prevailing wage rates when executing infrastructure contracts with public funds. New Jersey has a similar requirement for working with that state's Housing Finance Authority to finance affordable housing. In some states, Davis Bacon/Prevailing Wage hourly rates are close to union labor rates.

Local Hiring

Although it's hard to facilitate, the private and the public entities must make sure residents enjoy the financial ramifications of investments into their community. An 18-year-old should have an opportunity to apply for an entry-level position. A 30-year-old should have a chance to start a new career by achieving training and certification positions such as plumbing, electrical work, bricklaying, or road work.

Cities want dynamic and deep community connections. Creating financially stable constituents will accomplish that.

DESIGN

PUBLIC HOUSING AND AFFORDABLE HOUSING

When I was in undergrad learning how to design buildings in architecture school, I remember asking myself why there is no focus on creating innovation for all housing. We as designers fantasized about receiving massive commissions, those once in a lifetime projects for many architects in the midcentury, public housing provided that large scale once in a lifetime commission.

In the middle of the century (1940-1960s), Modern architecture was the design of choice at the time and became the signature look on public housing. This style emphasizes form over ornamentation. It shows an appreciation of materials and structure, in a minimalistic approach.

The epicenter of the Modernism was the Bauhaus. Bauhaus was a school of architecture, sculpture, and design in Germany. Walter Gropius led the school from 1919 to 1933. The talent from this place brought Modernism to the international stage. Gropius, along with the Marcel Breuer and Mies Van der Rhoe, left Germany in the late

1930s to escape nazi aggression. Gropius and Breuer became professors at Harvard University, and Mies became a professor at Chicago's Illinois Institute of Technology.

Many famous American architects such as Philip Johnson, Paul Rudolph, IM Pei, and Edward Durell Stone, were taught these modernist ideals, which have influenced Americans' cityscapes even today. Large concrete slabs with minimal ornamentation define the mid-20th-century architecture in America.

My favorite architect is Mies Van Der Rhoe; many would consider him the godfather of skyscrapers. His signature design is the use of exposed structures as a design decision.

The government primarily financed affordable housing or public housing in the 1940s - 1960s. The federal housing authority used modernist design principles in many of these massive urban design commissions.

Cite de Refuge in Paris was designed by one of the world's renowned architects, Charles-Édouard Jeanneret, also known as Le Corbusier, completed construction in 1933. This buildings' design is noteworthy because it used modern principles of exposed concrete structures on the exterior and interior spaces. This project was Le Corbusier's attempt to provide housing for the poor.

Many American cities over the next two decades pursue similar broad audacious design approaches. Because of a lack of continuous funding and support, many publicly financed affordable housing projects have fallen into severe disrepair.

Architects and urban planners today have moved away from this type of enormous resident warehousing solutions. Instead, today's approach mimics a more small scale, community-based, and community-engaged housing design. Today's workforce housing and affordable housing design are very often thought-provoking and creative. This trend will continue to repair communities for years to come.

SIGNATURE BUILDINGS AND STRUCTURES

In cities around the world, signature buildings attracts visitors and tourists. The ancient ruins in Greece are centuries old, but still have substantial demand for visitors each year. People travel to Las Vegas each year, not only for the pool parties and gambling, but also to take a photo in front of the bright lights in old downtown Las Vegas.

The Vessel structure at Hudson Yards New York is seeking similar fanfare, drawing tourists looking for their social media/cell phone photo glory. Tourism is the main economic driver in many localities. These structures of innovation are often produced by the private expertise.

PUBLIC SPACE

And lastly, parks and public space are an essential component of great cities and communities. Many studies confirm fresh air and tree-lined exterior spaces contribute to an improved quality of life. The government very often relies on private developers' participation in the creation and maintenance of these great exterior spaces, which become an extension of the city's living experiences.

Waterfront development has also grown significantly. As manufacturing and shipping have moved away from the need for waterway delivery, cities have begun to recapture that real estate for the betterment of the city after decades of decline. Some municipalities have created zoning bonuses for developers to create easily accessible public space on the waterfront. These include dog parks, playgrounds, and lawns.

A popular term in the urban planning realm currently is placemaking. The concept of placemaking is the idea of having a hands-on approach to improving a neighborhood, city, or region; this inspires participants to reimagine and reinvent public spaces as the center of the community. There are examples of significant public areas worldwide, such as the lawn in front of the Eiffel Tower, Bayfront Park in Miami, The National Mall in Washington DC, and Union Square in New York City. Many of the great spaces around today are a result of community-based participation. Along with designer/developer experience and knowledge. Great public space often increases the value of the real estate that surrounds it. These public spaces enhance the experience both physically, culturally, and socially for all.

CONCLUSION

What Should Private Parties Give Back to the Community?

Quality affordable and workforce housing should be available for teachers, nurses, accountants, cops, and firefighters. Excellent living conditions should also exist for our citizens with mental and physical impairments.

Private parties should facilitate the next healthy and sustained economic gain in a community; in simple terms, create good jobs. There are many proven ways to do this while earning a profit.

Private companies can create beautiful public spaces. This public-private partnership enhances the quality of life as well as property value in cities.

What Should Public Parties Give to the Community?

In most modern societies, citizens pay taxes in exchange for services that maintain a civil society. We really on the idea of safety and security for all.

I think something all national and local governments should be grappling with the reality that in 10 years, we'll rely more on technology performance and less on human labor. In other words, we'll need fewer people working in labor-intensive jobs and service jobs. We must prepare to provide a quality of life for our population in that future reality.

CLOSING THOUGHTS

I love to learn. And I love to teach. Hopefully, you learned a few new things or refreshed your knowledge with my books.

If you have thoughts or suggestions, please reach me at delainepublishing@gmail.com.

GLOSSARY

Green Construction – is a holistic concept that starts with the understanding that the built environment can have profound effects, both positive and negative, on the natural environment, as well as the people who inhabit buildings every day

Public-Private Real Estate Development – when the public parties and private parties work together using their resources for a common goal

Placemaking – is the idea of having a hands-on approach to improving a neighborhood, city or region

Real Estate Development - is the creation of value for real property

Tax Abatement – a reduced amount of real estate taxes

Subsidy – a benefit given to a business by the government in exchange for the promotion of some public good

www.ingramcontent.com/pod-product-compliance
Lightning Source LLC
Chambersburg PA
CBHW050306220526
45465CB00002B/840